WONDERFUL HOUSES
AROUND THE WORLD

YOSHIO KOMATSU

Drawings by Akira Nishiyama
Translated by Katy Bridges and Naoko Amemiya

Shelter Publications · Bolinas, California

WONDERFUL HOUSES
AROUND THE WORLD

*I like to photograph houses around the world.
I travel by airplane, car, bus, and boat to visit
any place with an interesting house. Wherever
I go, people I have never met before invite me
into their homes and offer me tea or a meal.
Let me show you some of the homes I have
visited and the way people live in them.*

—Yoshio Komatsu

Spain 26

Tunisia 22

Senegal 34

Togo 30

Bolivia 38

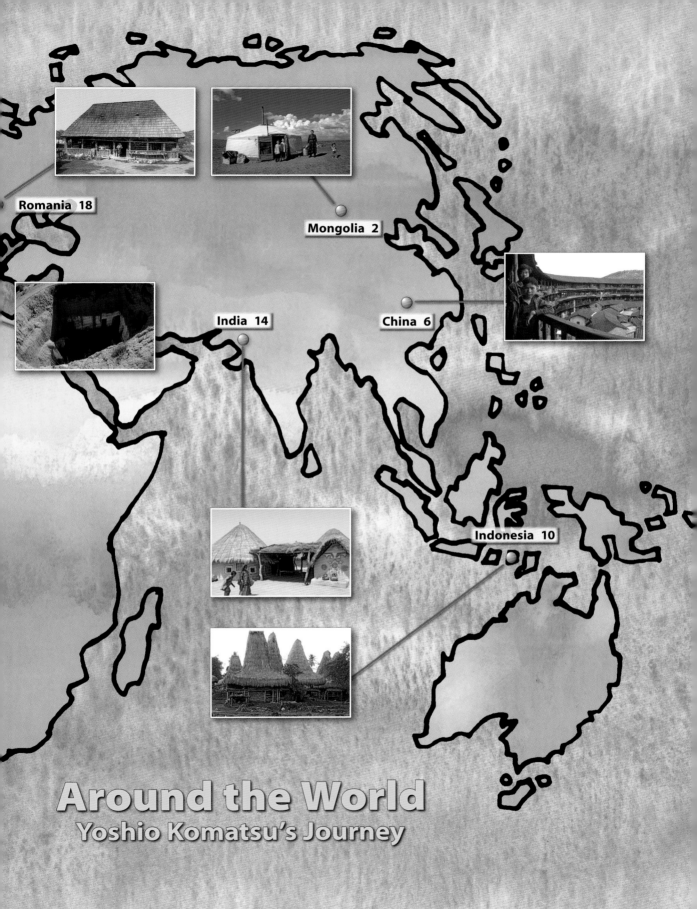

Romania 18

Mongolia 2

India 14

China 6

Indonesia 10

Around the World
Yoshio Komatsu's Journey

Mongolia
A White House in the Grasslands

THE GRASSLANDS CONTINUE AS FAR AS THE EYE CAN SEE. White specks dot the landscape here and there. As you get closer, you can see that these specks are actually houses. These are yurts (or *gers*), the portable, folding homes of people who live as herders of sheep and horses. Yurts are set up in places where water is easy to get, and where there is grass for the horses and sheep to eat.

When I visited this home on the steppe plateau of Tov Aimag, I was greeted with a big bowlful of *koumiss*, a fermented drink made from mare's milk. (A mare is a female horse.) When I finished one bowl, they poured me another. I ended up having four big bowls, or about half a gallon. The air is very dry here in Mongolia, and the *koumiss* made me feel very good.

Who lives here?
A father, a mother, and three children

FAMILY ALTAR

HORSE DROPPINGS ARE USED AS FUEL FOR THE STOVE.

THE OUTSIDE IS COVERED IN FELT.

THE FRAMEWORK OF THE HOUSE IS MADE OF
WOOD. AFTER THE FRAMEWORK IS SET UP, IT IS
COVERED WITH FELT MADE FROM SHEEPS' WOOL.
ONCE THE FELT IS TIED DOWN, THE HOUSE IS
FINISHED. WHEN IT IS TIME TO MOVE, IT IS
TAKEN APART AND MOVED ON HORSEBACK.

CHILDREN LEARN TO RIDE HORSES WHEN
THEY ARE ABOUT FOUR YEARS OLD.

KOUMISS, A
BEVERAGE
MADE FROM
MARE'S MILK

HAVING A FOAL NEARBY AT
MILKING TIME ENCOURAGES
THE MARE TO GIVE MORE MILK.

China
Living Together in a Circle

DEEP IN THE MOUNTAINS, there is a round earthen building called a *tulou*. It is surrounded by a thick dirt wall. It looks as if a huge flying saucer has landed. It is in the Fujian province of China.

There are as many as three hundred people living in this tulou. Entering through the gate in the wall, you will find it is very lively inside. Take a few steps, and here and there you will hear people calling to you to stop for tea. In the middle is the hall for ancestor worship. Looking up, you can see a round circle of sky.

Who lives here?
300 people!

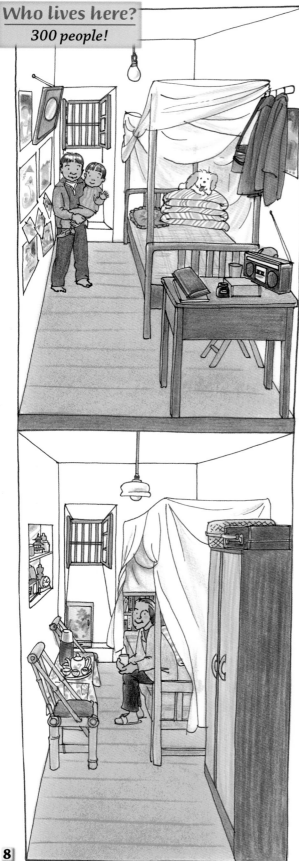

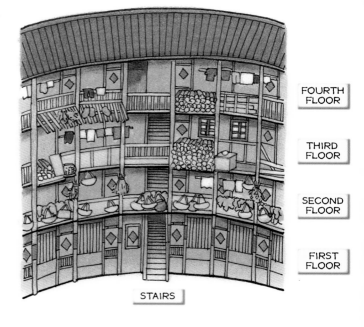

FOURTH FLOOR

THIRD FLOOR

SECOND FLOOR

FIRST FLOOR

STAIRS

THE *TULOU* HAS FOUR FLOORS. THERE ARE FOUR COMMUNAL STAIRCASES, AND MORE THAN 200 ROOMS OF ABOUT THE SAME SIZE. ON THE FIRST FLOOR THERE ARE KITCHENS ALL IN A ROW. ALONG THE CORRIDOR THERE ARE ALSO OUTDOOR COOKING STOVES, WHERE PEOPLE CAN STAND AND EAT CASUALLY. ON THE INSIDE OF THE CORRIDOR IS WHERE PIGS, RABBITS, CHICKENS, AND DUCKS ARE KEPT. *(SEE PAGE ON RIGHT.)* THE SECOND FLOOR HAS THE WAREHOUSES, WHERE THE HARVEST AND THE FARM TOOLS ARE KEPT. THE LONG HALL IS WHERE THE CHILDREN PLAY. *(SEE BELOW.)* THE THIRD AND FOURTH FLOORS HAVE BEDROOMS THAT ARE ALSO USED FOR STUDY. PARENTS AND CHILDREN SHARE ONE ROOM. *(SEE LEFT.)*

9

Indonesia
Houses with Pointed Roofs

THESE HOUSES ON SUMBA ISLAND, INDONESIA are made from bamboo and grass. Livestock, such as water buffalo and pigs, live under the raised floor, and the people live above. The pointed part of the roof is where the gods are said to live.

The sun has set, so it is time to fetch the water buffalo that have been grazing on grass in the meadow, and bring them back under the floor.

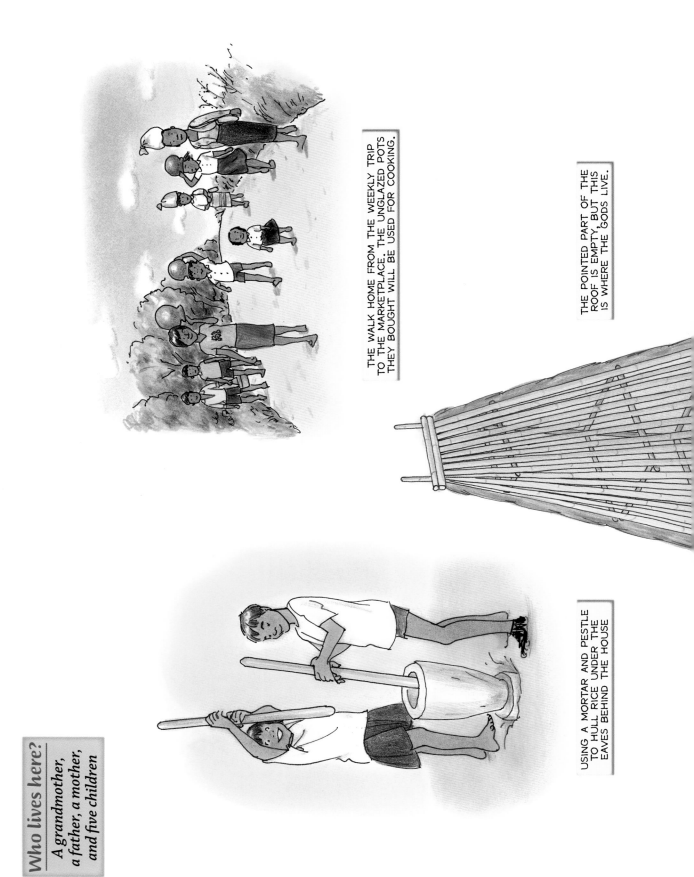

Who lives here?

A grandmother, a father, a mother, and five children

THE WALK HOME FROM THE WEEKLY TRIP TO THE MARKETPLACE. THE UNGLAZED POTS THEY BOUGHT WILL BE USED FOR COOKING.

THE POINTED PART OF THE ROOF IS EMPTY, BUT THIS IS WHERE THE GODS LIVE.

USING A MORTAR AND PESTLE TO HULL RICE UNDER THE EAVES BEHIND THE HOUSE

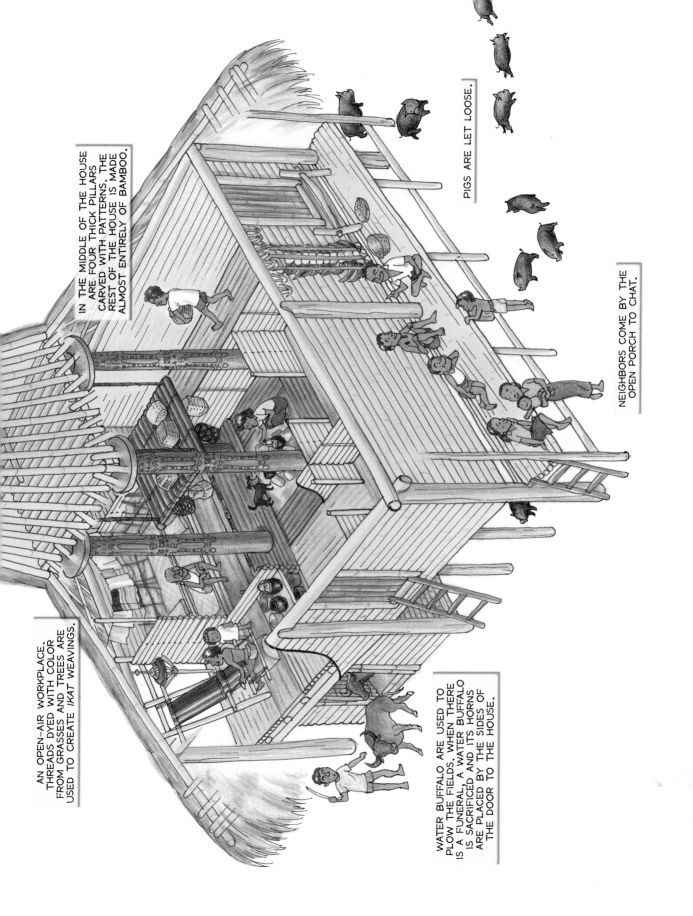

IN THE MIDDLE OF THE HOUSE ARE FOUR THICK PILLARS CARVED WITH PATTERNS. THE REST OF THE HOUSE IS MADE ALMOST ENTIRELY OF BAMBOO.

PIGS ARE LET LOOSE.

NEIGHBORS COME BY THE OPEN PORCH TO CHAT.

AN OPEN-AIR WORKPLACE. THREADS DYED WITH COLOR FROM GRASSES AND TREES ARE USED TO CREATE IKAT WEAVINGS.

WATER BUFFALO ARE USED TO PLOW THE FIELDS. WHEN THERE IS A FUNERAL, A WATER BUFFALO IS SACRIFICED AND ITS HORNS ARE PLACED BY THE SIDES OF THE DOOR TO THE HOUSE.

India
Houses Wearing Hats

THE WIND BLOWS THROUGH HERE. Shortly after noon, the wind from the ocean in the south comes blowing through this area towards the desert in the north. This house is in the Kutch region of India. Its roof is firmly tied down with rope so that it does not blow away in the wind.

The grass roof and the earthen walls block the heat outside. The women draw designs on the outside walls. The inside of the house is also elaborately decorated.

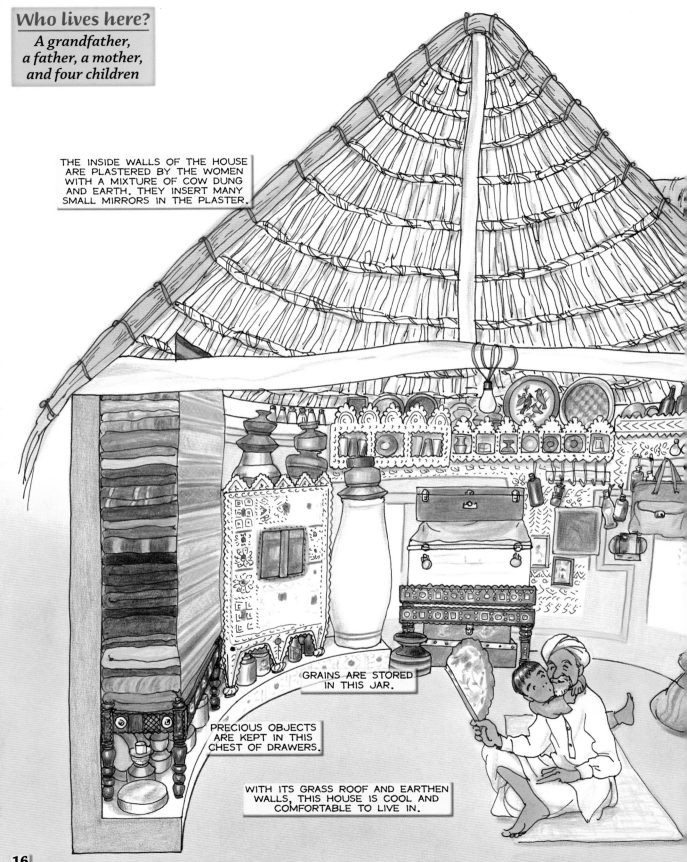

Who lives here?

*A grandfather,
a father, a mother,
and four children*

THE INSIDE WALLS OF THE HOUSE ARE PLASTERED BY THE WOMEN WITH A MIXTURE OF COW DUNG AND EARTH. THEY INSERT MANY SMALL MIRRORS IN THE PLASTER.

GRAINS ARE STORED IN THIS JAR.

PRECIOUS OBJECTS ARE KEPT IN THIS CHEST OF DRAWERS.

WITH ITS GRASS ROOF AND EARTHEN WALLS, THIS HOUSE IS COOL AND COMFORTABLE TO LIVE IN.

16

WATER IS DRAWN FROM WELLS, AND IS KEPT IN UNGLAZED POTS. WHEN THE WATER THAT SEEPS OUT OF AN UNGLAZED POT EVAPORATES, IT DRAWS OUT HEAT, COOLING THE WATER INSIDE.

COOKING STOVE

UNGLAZED WATER POT

A BED WITH LONG LEGS. THE DISTANCE FROM THE HOT GROUND HELPS TO KEEP IT COOL.

THE WOMEN WORK ON EMBROIDERY, SEWING SMALL MIRRORS ONTO FABRIC.

Romania
A House with Eyes in Its Roof

THIS VILLAGE IS IN A CLEARING by a forest full of fir and oak in the Maramures region of Romania. Here, even the roofs of the houses are made of wooden shingles. As I walked through the village, I felt as if someone was always watching me.

It was the eyes on the roofs of the houses. The openings look just like human eyes complete with eyelids, but are actually holes to let smoke escape.

Who lives here?

A grandmother, a father, a mother, and three children

THE ROOF IS STEEPLY SLOPED BECAUSE IT SNOWS A LOT IN WINTER.

SMOKE HOLE

PEOPLE IN THIS REGION KEEP A LOT OF SHEEP. WOMEN MAKE YARN FROM SHEEPS' WOOL WHEN THEIR OTHER JOBS ARE FINISHED.

MAKING PICKLES IN PREPARATION FOR WINTER

THE SPACE UNDER THE ROOF IS USED FOR FOOD STORAGE. THE SMOKE FROM THE KITCHEN OVEN FILLS THIS SPACE, WHICH MAKES IT GOOD FOR PRESERVING FOOD. CORN, SALTED MEAT, AND SAUSAGES ARE STORED HERE.

WATER IS DRAWN FROM THE WELL.

JUST-WASHED DISHES ARE HUNG ON THE BRANCHES OF DEAD TREES TO DRY.

Tunisia
Living Underground

IF YOU CLIMB A SMALL HILL AND LOOK DOWN at the village of Matmata, you might notice there are many holes that look like craters on the moon. These holes are actually houses. The bottoms of the holes are the courtyards of the houses, and the holes dug off to the sides of the courtyards are rooms.

23

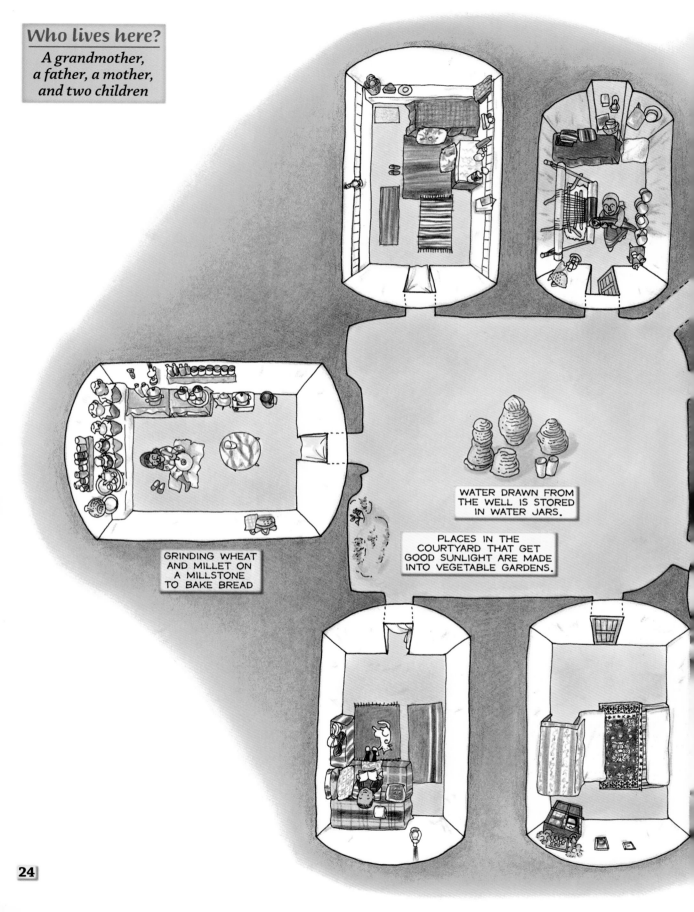

Who lives here?
A grandmother,
a father, a mother,
and two children

GRINDING WHEAT
AND MILLET ON
A MILLSTONE
TO BAKE BREAD

WATER DRAWN FROM
THE WELL IS STORED
IN WATER JARS.

PLACES IN THE
COURTYARD THAT GET
GOOD SUNLIGHT ARE MADE
INTO VEGETABLE GARDENS.

WELLS ARE LOCATED OUTSIDE THE HOUSE, SO THAT'S WHERE PEOPLE IN MATMATA DO THEIR LAUNDRY.

GRASS TO FEED TO THE GOATS IS CARRIED BY CAMELS.

TEMPERATURES IN SUMMER ARE CLOSE TO 120 DEGREES, AND IN WINTER, LESS THAN 32 DEGREES, BUT TEMPERATURES IN THE UNDERGROUND ROOMS ARE ALWAYS BETWEEN 70 TO 80 DEGREES ALL YEAR, AND COMFORTABLE. THERE IS NOT MUCH RAINFALL AND THE SOIL DRAINS WELL, SO WATER DOES NOT GET INTO THE ROOMS. IF A FAMILY GETS BIGGER AND NEEDS MORE SPACE, THEY DIG OUT ANOTHER ROOM. AFTER PLASTERING THE ENTRANCE AND WALLS WHITE, THE NEW ROOM IS READY.

Spain
Houses that Breathe
Through Chimneys

MANY WHITE CHIMNEYS SPRING OUT OF THE GROUND! I wanted to see one of the chimneys up closer, so I climbed up the hill that it was coming out of. I felt as if my footsteps were echoing underground. When I walked softly down the other side of the hill, I found the entrance to a house. An elderly couple saw me wandering around and invited me in. These underground houses are in Gaudix, Spain.

Who lives here?

A grandfather and grandmother. (Their two children are grown and have moved to the city.)

ROOMS IN THESE HOMES ARE CARVED OUT OF ROCKY HILLS AND CLIFFS. ROOMS ARE BUILT WITH GENTLY DOME-SHAPED CEILINGS BECAUSE THIS SHAPE IS STRONG AND RARELY CAVES IN. ROOMS ARE PLASTERED ON THE INSIDE. WHEN INCREASING THE NUMBER OF ROOMS, YOU MUST BE CAREFUL NOT TO BREAK THROUGH TO THE HOUSE NEXT DOOR!

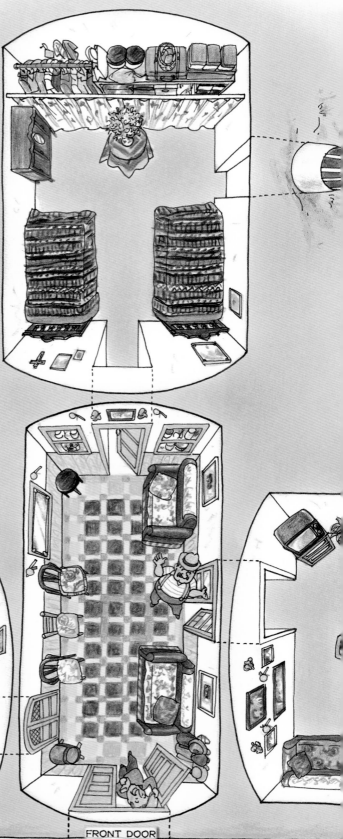

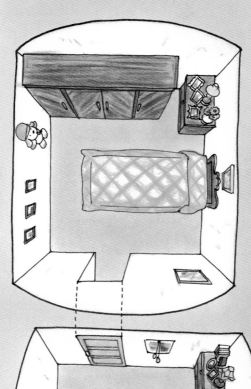

FRONT DOOR

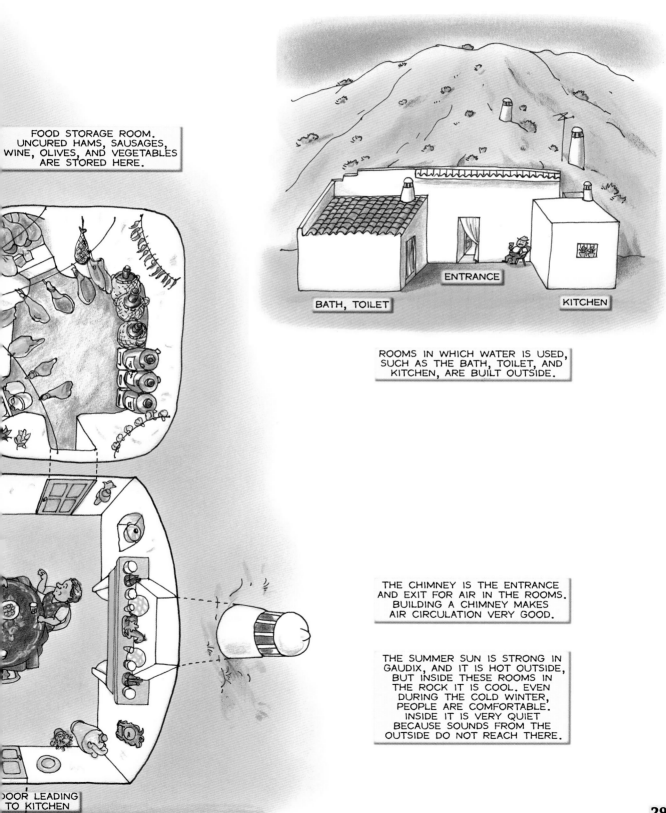

FOOD STORAGE ROOM. UNCURED HAMS, SAUSAGES, WINE, OLIVES, AND VEGETABLES ARE STORED HERE.

BATH, TOILET

ENTRANCE

KITCHEN

ROOMS IN WHICH WATER IS USED, SUCH AS THE BATH, TOILET, AND KITCHEN, ARE BUILT OUTSIDE.

THE CHIMNEY IS THE ENTRANCE AND EXIT FOR AIR IN THE ROOMS. BUILDING A CHIMNEY MAKES AIR CIRCULATION VERY GOOD.

THE SUMMER SUN IS STRONG IN GAUDIX, AND IT IS HOT OUTSIDE, BUT INSIDE THESE ROOMS IN THE ROCK IT IS COOL. EVEN DURING THE COLD WINTER, PEOPLE ARE COMFORTABLE. INSIDE IT IS VERY QUIET BECAUSE SOUNDS FROM THE OUTSIDE DO NOT REACH THERE.

DOOR LEADING TO KITCHEN

A house made of mud stands close to a large Baobab tree in the Tamberma region of Togo, Africa.

Who lives here?

A grandmother, a father, two children and their mother, and three children and their mother

DRYING BEANS AND CHILI PEPPERS ON THE ROOFTOP

HOLES FOR LOOKING OUTSIDE

BEDROOM

SMALL SHRINES REPRESENT EACH FAMILY MEMBER.

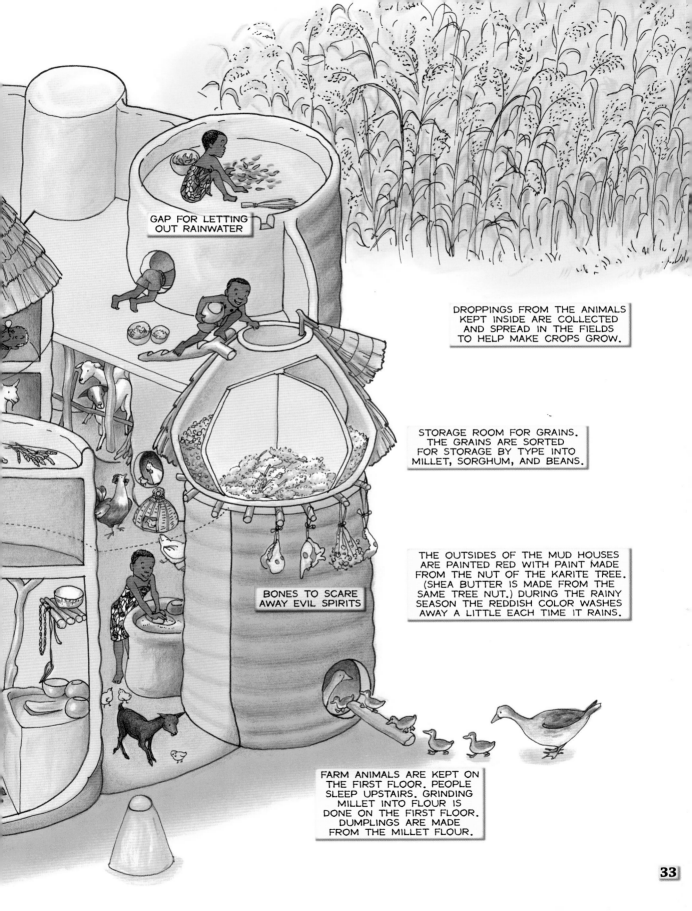

GAP FOR LETTING OUT RAINWATER

DROPPINGS FROM THE ANIMALS KEPT INSIDE ARE COLLECTED AND SPREAD IN THE FIELDS TO HELP MAKE CROPS GROW.

STORAGE ROOM FOR GRAINS. THE GRAINS ARE SORTED FOR STORAGE BY TYPE INTO MILLET, SORGHUM, AND BEANS.

THE OUTSIDES OF THE MUD HOUSES ARE PAINTED RED WITH PAINT MADE FROM THE NUT OF THE KARITE TREE. (SHEA BUTTER IS MADE FROM THE SAME TREE NUT.) DURING THE RAINY SEASON THE REDDISH COLOR WASHES AWAY A LITTLE EACH TIME IT RAINS.

BONES TO SCARE AWAY EVIL SPIRITS

FARM ANIMALS ARE KEPT ON THE FIRST FLOOR. PEOPLE SLEEP UPSTAIRS. GRINDING MILLET INTO FLOUR IS DONE ON THE FIRST FLOOR. DUMPLINGS ARE MADE FROM THE MILLET FLOUR.

Senegal
Is This Roof Upside Down?

THE HOUSE IN THE CENTER OF THE VILLAGE COLLECTS rainwater inside the home to use as drinking water. This is because even when wells are dug, the water is salty.

I wanted to see what the roof looked like, so I got a ride in an airplane to fly overhead and look at it. These houses are in the Casamance region of Senegal, Africa.

Who lives here?
A grandfather, a grandmother, a father, three children and their mother, and four children and their mother

THE ROOF IS HELD UP BY THE TRUNKS OF MANGROVE TREES. MANY MANGROVE TREES ARE FOUND IN THIS AREA.

BASKET TRAPS FOR CATCHING FISH

MAKING SOUP FROM OYSTERS FOUND ON THE ROOTS OF MANGROVE TREES

THERE ARE FOUR ROOMS AROUND THIS ROOM.

SEWING IS MEN'S WORK.

MORTAR AND PESTLE
USED FOR HULLING RICE

Bolivia
Houses Shaped Like Acorns

THE CHIPAYA PEOPLE live on a plateau in the Andes at an elevation of 10,000 feet above sea level. If you listen carefully, you can hear the faint sound of a stream. White crystallized salt rises to float on the surface of the damp earth near the stream.

There is a grass that grows in this earth where there is so much salt. Sheep and llamas eat this grass. The Chipaya people cut blocks out of this root-bound earth and stack them to build their acorn-shaped houses.

Who lives here?

A father, a mother, and three children

THE BLOCKS ARE STACKED IN CIRCLES THAT GET SMALLER AND SMALLER. DOING THIS IS AN EASY WAY TO MAKE A STURDY STRUCTURE.

MAKING QUINOA PORRIDGE

BLOCKS OF ROOT-BOUND EARTH ARE USED FOR BUILDING HOUSES BECAUSE PEOPLE CAN CUT AND MAKE MANY SUCH BLOCKS ANYWHERE IN THIS AREA.

THE WALLS OF THE SHEEP PEN ARE ALSO MADE OF EARTHEN BLOCKS. THIS WORKS BECAUSE THE SHEEP DO NOT EAT THE ROOTS.

QUINOA IS A GRAIN THAT CAN BE GROWN EVEN IN AN AREA WITH POOR SOIL. HERE THE WOMAN IS POURING THE MILLET AND LETTING THE WIND BLOW AWAY THE CHAFF (THE PART OF THE MILLET YOU CANNOT EAT).

OUTDOOR COOKING OVEN

41

A ROAD SIGN IN THE
DESERT READING
"LEFT TO MATMATA"

The houses shown in this book are only a small number
of the houses I have visited. There are many other
interesting houses all over the world—more than I
could ever visit and photograph. To me, these houses
are very beautiful. I hope to keep photographing wonderful houses around the world for a long time to come.

About the Author

YOSHIO KOMATSU has travelled all over the world for the past 25 years, shooting pictures of simple homes and the people that live in them. He has published several books in Japanese, including *Living on Earth*. His first book in English, *Built By Hand: Vernacular Buildings Around the World*, was published by Gibbs Smith in 2003. Yoshio's photographs appear frequently in magazines and calendars in Japan, as well as in books. His wife, artist **EIKO KOMATSU**, often travels with him, and she did the preliminary drawings for the houses shown in this book. Yoshio and Eiko, when not travelling, live in Tokyo, Japan.

AKIRA NISHIYAMA studied at the Joshibi University of Art and Design in Tokyo. She has done essays and illustrations for lifestyle magazines and books, including *Treasure Box for Wonderful Living* and *Coordinate Book*.

Distributed in the United States by Publishers Group West and in Canada by Publishers Group Canada.

Original version: Text and photographs by Yoshio Komatsu, © 1997. Drawings by Akira Nishiyama, © 1997.

Originally published under the title of *The Wonderful Houses Around the World* (Sekai Achikochi Yukaina Ie Meguri) by Fukuinkan-Shoten Publishers, Inc., Tokyo, Japan

LIBRARY OF CONGRESS CATALOGING-IN-PUBLICATION DATA

Komatsu, Yoshio, 1945–
  Wonderful houses around the world / Yoshio Komatsu.
    p.   cm.
  ISBN-10: 0-936070-35-8 — ISBN-13: 978-0-936070-35-3
  ISBN-10: 0-936070-34-X (pbk.) — ISBN-13: 978-0-936070-34-6 (pbk.)
  1. Architecture, Domestic.   I. Title.
N7110.K64 2004
728'.37 — dc22

                                                          2004016240

7 6 5 4 3 — 11 10 09

(Lowest digits indicate number and year of latest printing.)
Printed in China

Shelter Publications, Inc.
P.O. Box 279
Bolinas, California 94924
415-868-0280
Orders, toll-free: 1-800-307-0131